# Maths made Merry

## Workbook Grade 3

Om KIDZ
An imprint of Om Books International

# NUMBER WHOPPER

Help the aliens write the names of the numbers given below.

342

425

754

234

596

845

# NUMBER LADDER

Arnold the Astroboy is building a star path, but got the numbers mixed up. Can you arrange them in an ascending order?

# BACK TO EARTH

Annie the Astrogirl is coming home after a long space tour, but her number paths got jumbled again. Can you sort these out in a descending order?

| 361 | |
|---|---|
| 215 | |
| 121 | |
| 152 | |
| 742 | |

| 521 | |
|---|---|
| 247 | |
| 719 | |
| 417 | |
| 344 | |

| 248 | |
|---|---|
| 489 | |
| 942 | |
| 847 | |
| 175 | |

# EXPANDING ALIENS

These aliens are getting to know numbers. Can you write the expanded form of the numbers below?

251 = ____________________

710 = ____________________

888 = ____________________

967 = ____________________

123 = ____________________

435 = ____________________

# PREDECESSORS AND SUCCESSORS

Professor Spaceman is teaching the aliens about predecessors and successors. Read the numbers below and fill in the table correctly.

| Predecessor | Number | Successor |
|---|---|---|
| 244 | 245 | |
| | 465 | 466 |
| | 344 | |
| | 774 | |
| | 578 | |
| | 800 | |

# SPACE MAZE

Help the aliens reach their spaceship by following the path with the correct number order.

# PATTERNED PATHS

Read the numbers on the starry paths and fill in the correct number to complete the pattern.

101, 103, 105, 107, ____, ____, ____

122, 124, 126, 128, ____, ____, ____

450, 455, 460, 465, ____, ____, ____

314, 319, 324, 329, ____, ____, ____

231 234 237 240 ___ ___ ___

600 606 612 618 ___ ___ ___

107 114 121 128 ___ ___ ___

510 515 520 525 ___ ___ ___

# WORDY WOES

Let's solve the word problems on the planets below.

Alien X bought 739 chocolates. His human friend Annie bought 596. Who has more chocolates?

Allie the Alien has 565 eyes. Her sister Abbie has 656 eyes. Who has lesser eyes?

Mongo the Alien blew up 909 asteroids. His brother Bongo blew up 909. Who blew up more?

Arnold the Astronaut flew past 489 stars during his space tour. His friend Barney flew past 498. Who saw more stars?

# SHAPELY MATCH

Help the alien match these shapes to their correct names.

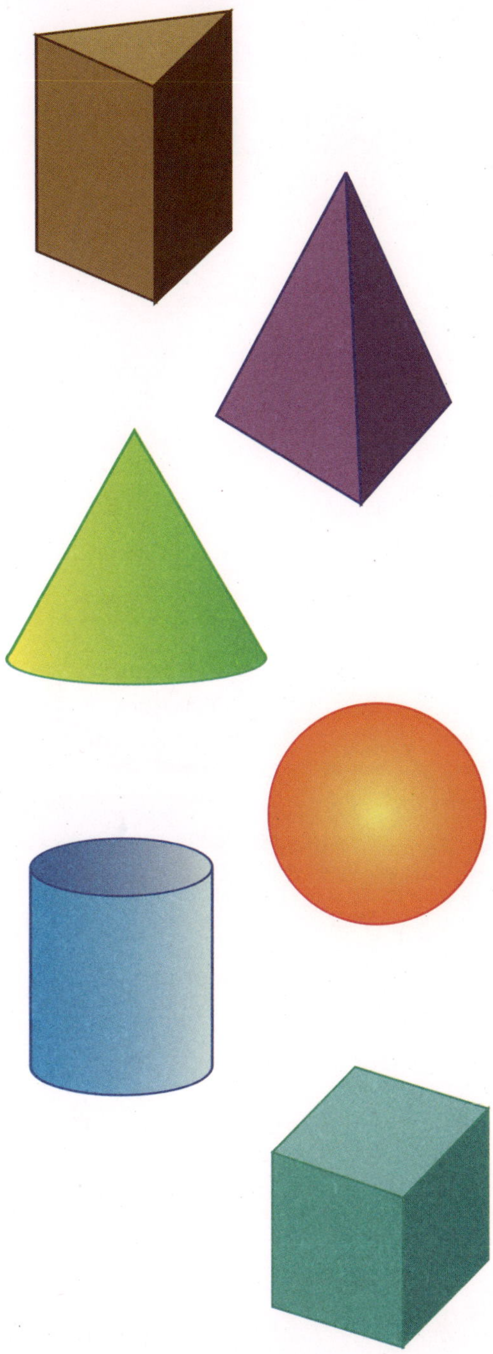

cylinder

sphere

prism

cube

pyramid

cone

# METEORITE MATH

Solve the sums on the meteorites to reach the Earth.

32 + 12 + 34 =

58 + 64 + 73 =

110 + 90 + 12 =

21 + 98 + 40 =

216 + 100 + 111 =

123 + 452 + 124 =

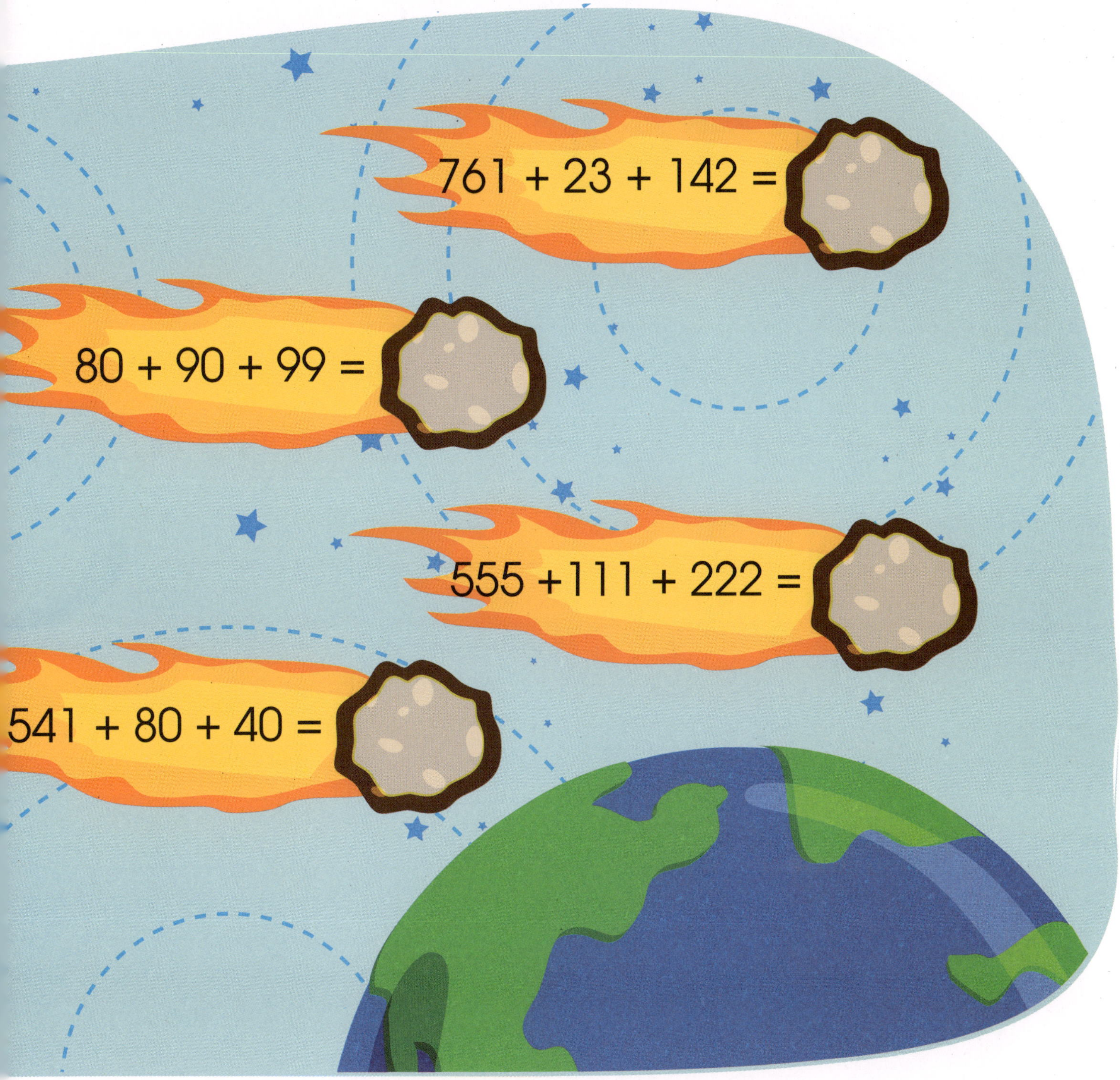
761 + 23 + 142 =
80 + 90 + 99 =
555 +111 + 222 =
541 + 80 + 40 =

# SUBTRACTING SPACESHIPS

Solve the sums on the spaceships and help Maximus the Alien reach its home planet.

70 – 44 =
58 – 27 =
71 – 19 =
82 – 16 =
HOME

# MENTAL MATH

Read the sums on the starry paths and try to solve them mentally.

If you take away 10 from the sum of 59 and 32, what do you get?

If you take away 12 from the sum of 62 and 27, what do you get?

If you take away 14 from the sum of 89 and 41, what do you get?

If you take away 26 from the sum of 95 and 26, what do you get?

# STARRY SURPRISE

Help Simpoo the Star solve the sums on the clouds.

5 x 3 =

7 x 4 =

10 x 3 =

4 x 5 =

8 x 8 =

9 x 6 =

9 x 2 =

7 x 7 =

# MULTIPLYING MONSTERS

Multiply the numbers on the comets to stop them from destroying our planet.

# DOTTO'S DILEMMA

Dotto the Alien wants to purchase some goodies but doesn't know how to count. Can you help to him count?

- If one bar of chocolate costs 20 rupees, what will the cost of 8 bars be?

- If one pencil costs 7 rupees, what will the cost of 14 pencils be?

- If one packet of chips costs 15 rupees, what will the cost of 17 packets be?

- If one notebook costs 12 rupees, what will the cost of 14 notebooks be?

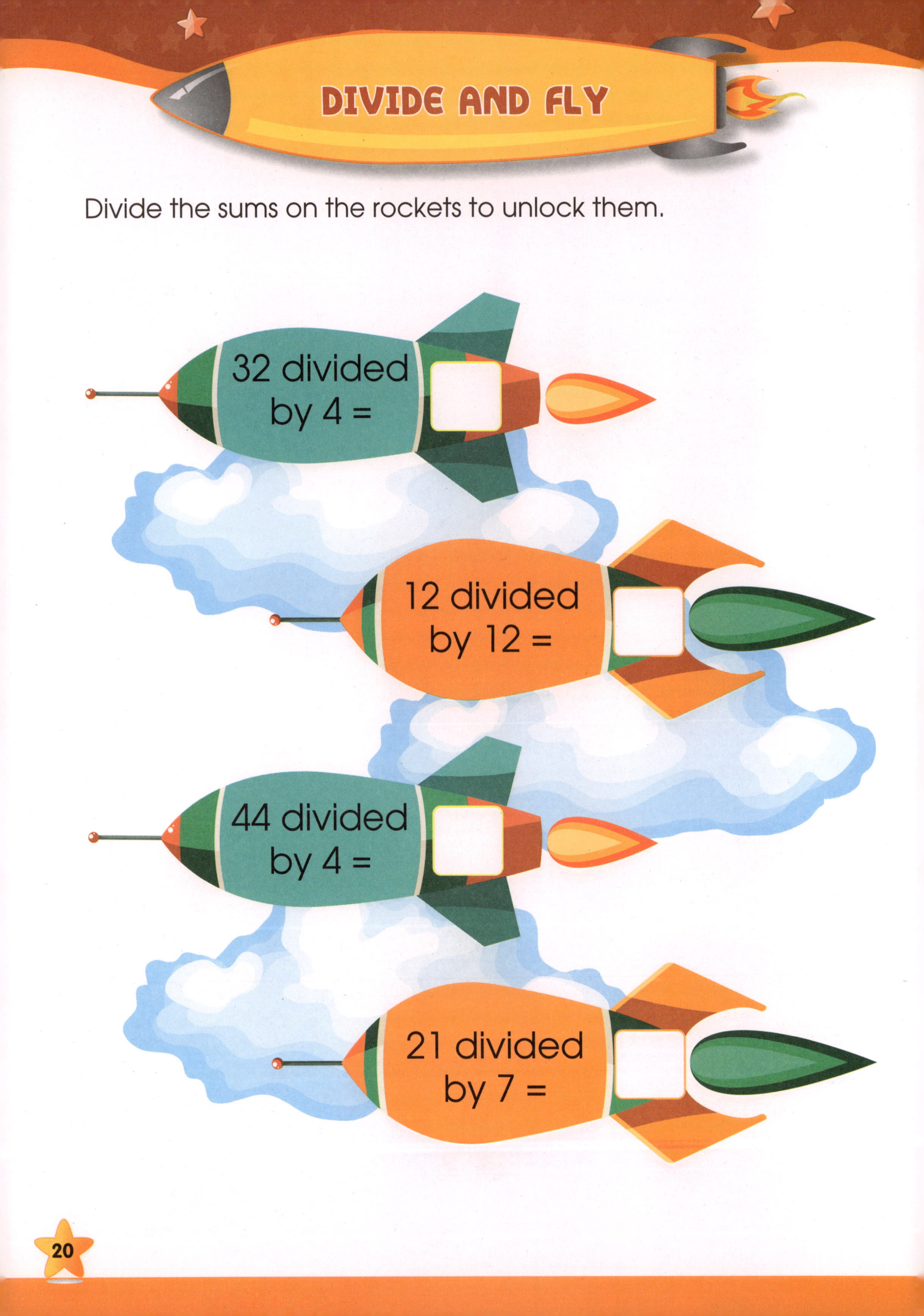

# DIVIDE AND FLY

Divide the sums on the rockets to unlock them.

32 divided by 4 = ☐

12 divided by 12 = ☐

44 divided by 4 = ☐

21 divided by 7 = ☐

64 divided by 8 =

25 divided by 5 =

28 divided by 4 =

# QUOTIENTS AND REMAINDERS

Solve the sums on the planets. Write the quotients and the remainders below.

21 ÷ 4

Quotient Remainder

89 ÷ 9

Quotient Remainder

97 ÷ 7

Quotient Remainder

124 ÷ 3

Quotient Remainder

45 ÷ 4

Quotient Remainder

$92 \div 3$

Quotient Remainder

$57 \div 6$

Quotient Remainder

$72 \div 7$

Quotient Remainder

$92 \div 4$

Quotient Remainder

$65 \div 8$

Quotient Remainder

# CLOUDED CALCULATIONS

Divide the sums on the clouds.

$\frac{55}{5} = \square$

$\frac{84}{4} = \square$

$\frac{69}{3} = \square$

$\frac{60}{3} = \square$

$\frac{78}{3} = \square$

$\frac{46}{2} = \square$

# FRACTIONED PLANETS

Read the fraction below the planets. Divide each planet and colour them according to the fraction.

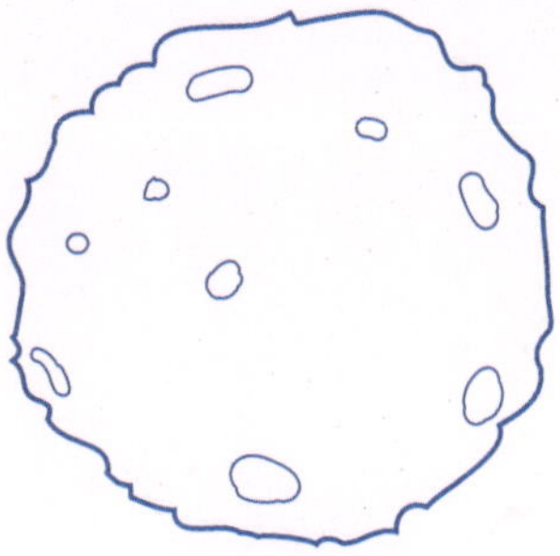

$\frac{4}{5}$

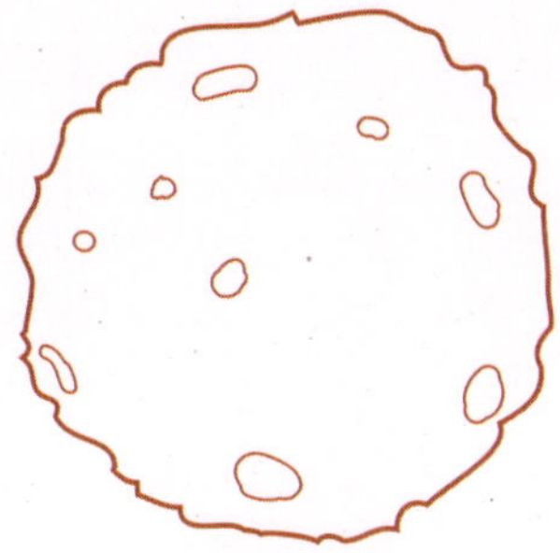

$\frac{3}{8}$

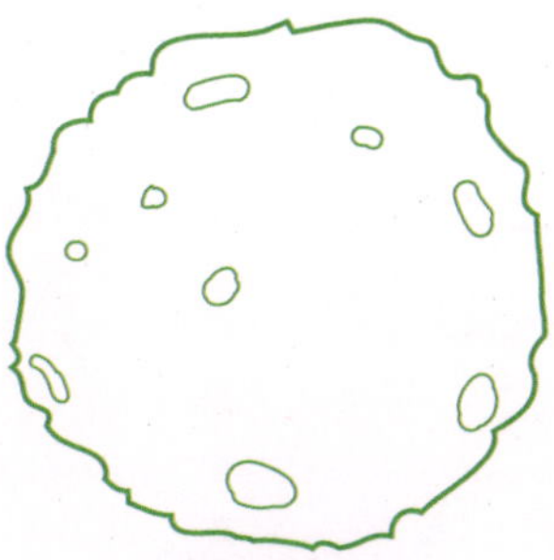

$\frac{1}{3}$

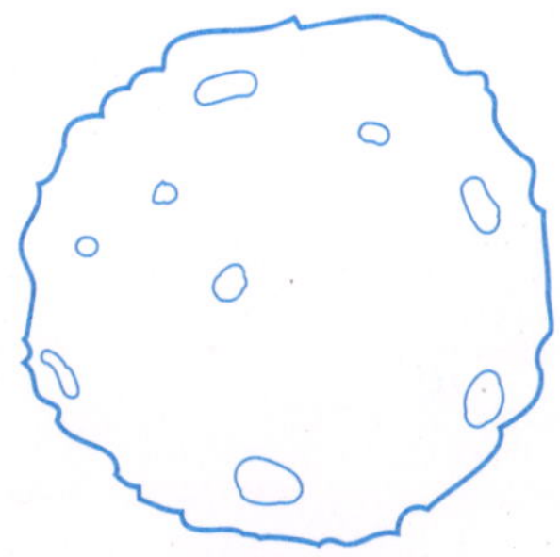

$\frac{2}{3}$

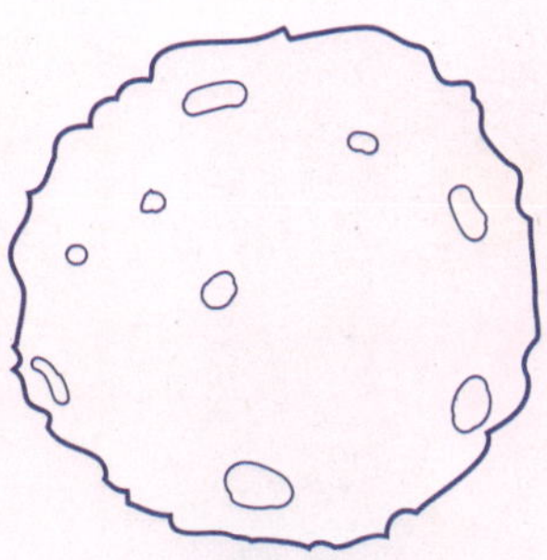

$\frac{5}{7}$

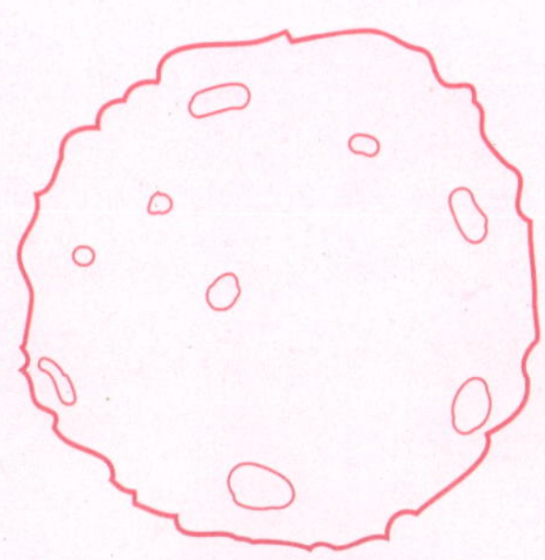

$\frac{1}{6}$

# FRACTIONED FLAG

Solve the fraction sums on the flag below.

$$\frac{1}{3} + \frac{1}{3} =$$

$$\frac{1}{4} + \frac{2}{4} =$$

$$\frac{1}{9} + \frac{7}{9} =$$

$$\frac{5}{6} + \frac{1}{6} =$$

$$\frac{3}{8} + \frac{2}{8} =$$

$$\frac{1}{5} + \frac{3}{5} =$$

# CLOCKS

Look at the time below the clocks and draw their hands accordingly.

10:57

9:07

4:26

6:34

2:21

12:00

# MONEY MATH

Help the aliens convert the following dollars to cents.

# MEASURING MAYHEM

Help Robo the Alien learn about measurements by following the instructions below.

Circle the spaceship that looks heavier.

Circle the longer rocket.

Circle the planet with more water in it.

# NUMBER PATHWAY

Help Annie the Astrogirl meet her alien friends by numbering the pathway correctly.

# ANSWERS

## Page 2

## Page 3

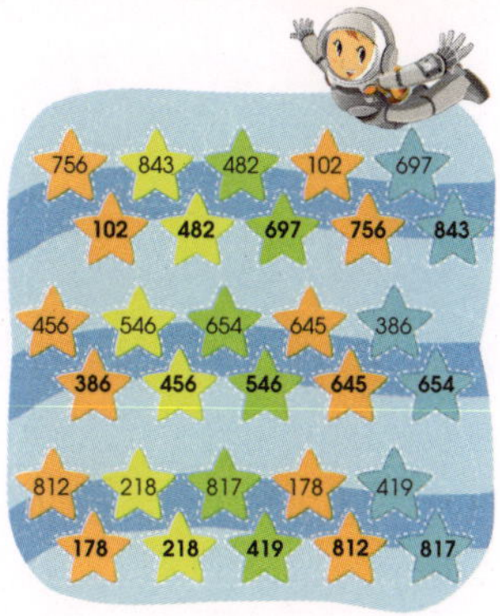


## Page 4

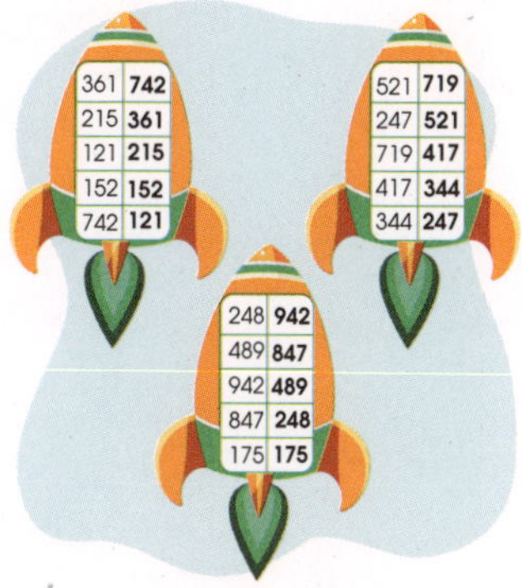


## Page 5

## Page 6

## Page 7

## Page 8

## Page 9

## Page 10

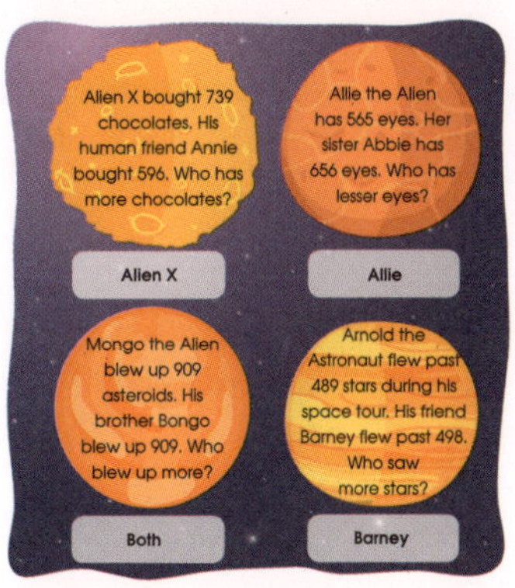


## Page 11

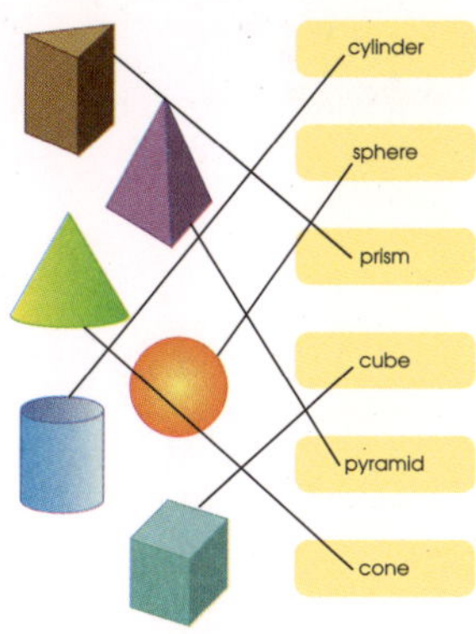


## Page 12

## Page 13

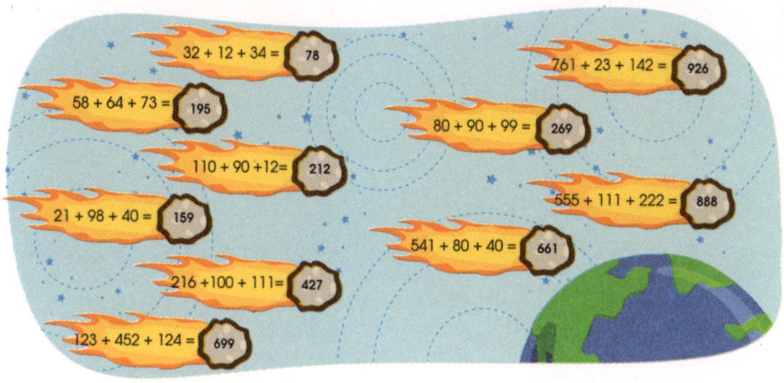


## Page 14

## Page 15

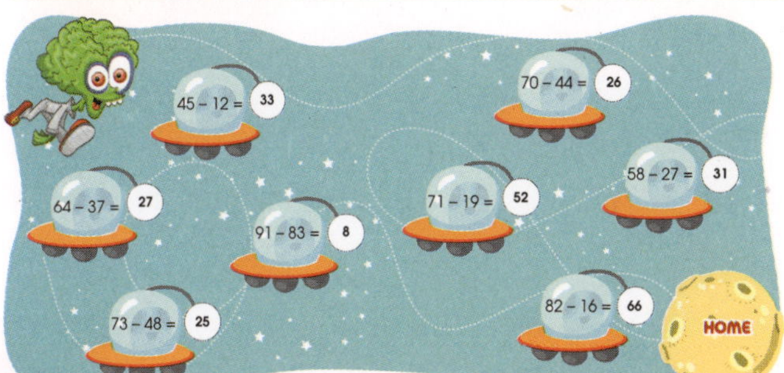


## Page 16

## Page 17

# ANSWERS

## Page 18

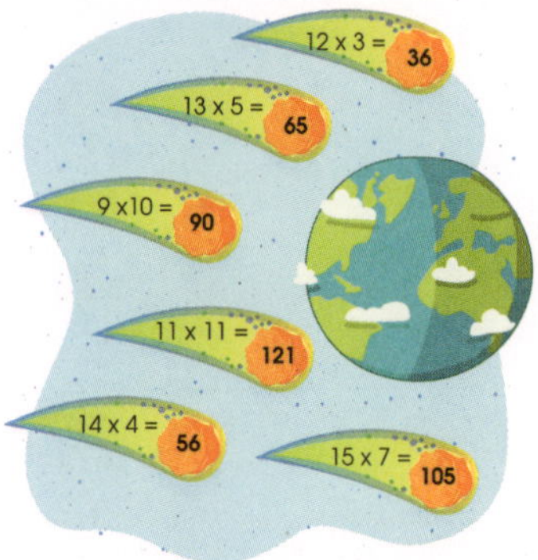


## Page 19

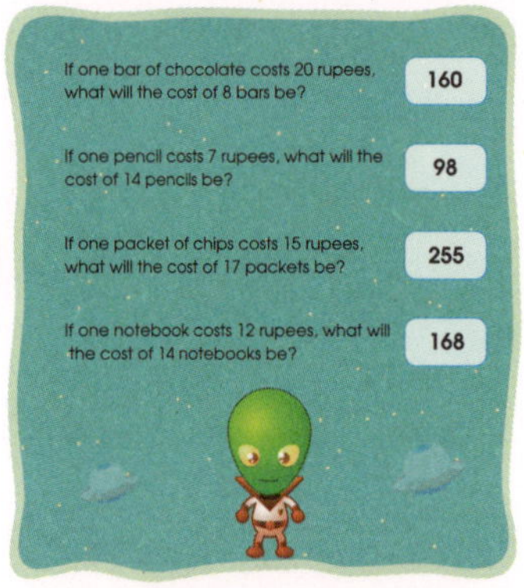


## Page 20

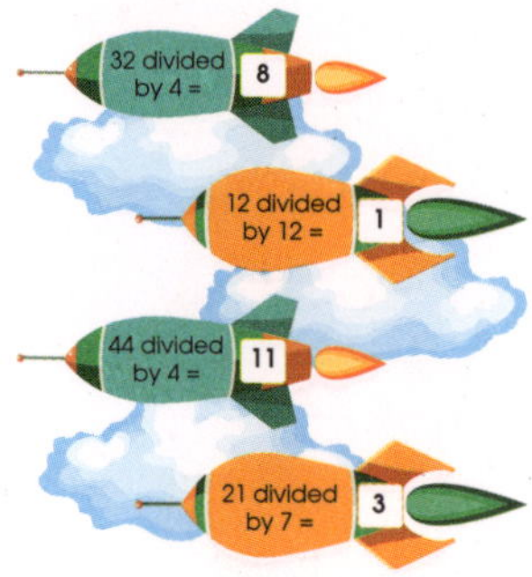


## Page 21

## Page 22

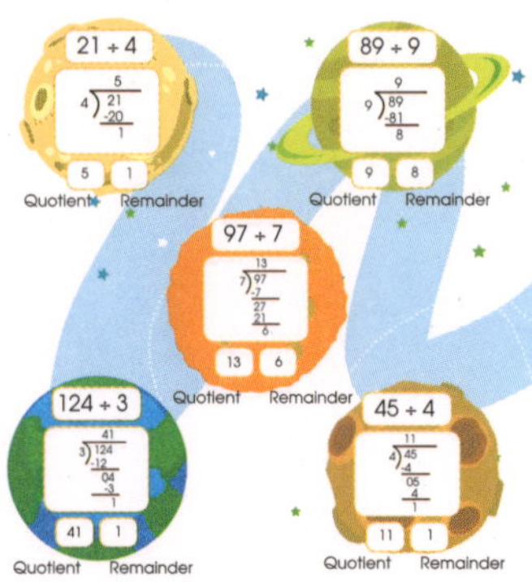


## Page 23

## Page 24

## Page 25

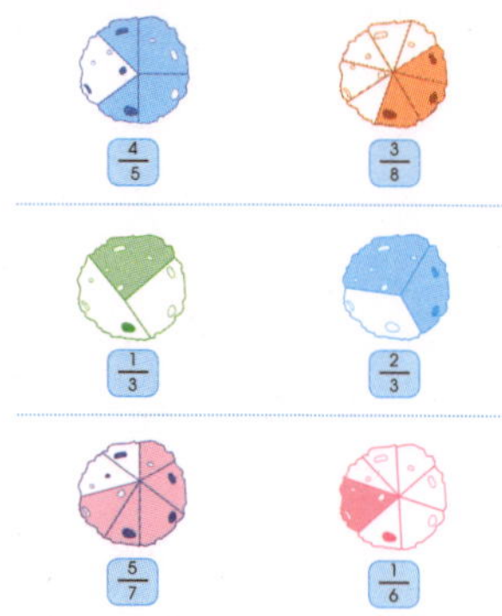


## Page 26

## Page 27

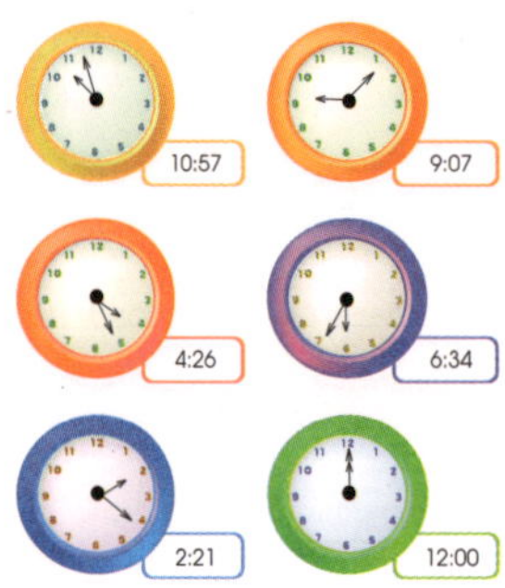


## Page 28

## Page 29

## Page 30